"Maximizing Your Social Media Income: Tips and Tricks for Earnings"

Introduction

Welcome to "Maximizing Your Social Media Income: Tips and Tricks for Earnings." In the digital age, social media platforms are not just for connecting with friends or sharing personal updates—they have become powerful tools for generating income. Whether you're an influencer, a business owner, or just someone looking to make extra money online, this ebook will guide you through the myriad ways to monetise your social media presence effectively.

In this comprehensive guide, we will explore proven strategies for increasing your follower count, engaging with your audience, and turning your social media activity into a profitable venture. From understanding algorithms and mastering content creation to leveraging sponsorships and affiliate marketing, we cover it all. You'll also find insights on choosing the right platforms for your niche, setting realistic financial goals, and measuring your success.

With practical tips and real-world examples, this ebook aims to equip you with the knowledge and tools needed to thrive in the competitive world of social media marketing. Start your journey towards financial independence and discover how to turn your online presence into a steady income stream. Let's unlock the potential of your social media channels together.

Index

1. **Create Quality Content**: Consistently produce high-quality, engaging content that resonates with your audience.

2. **Utilize Multiple Platforms**: Diversify your presence across different social media platforms to reach a broader audience.
3. **Engage with Your Followers**: Interact with your audience through comments, messages, and live sessions to build a loyal community.
4. **Use Hashtags Strategically**: Employ relevant hashtags to increase your content's visibility and reach.
5. **Collaborate with Influencers**: Partner with other influencers to expand your reach and gain new followers.
6. **Monetise with Ads**: Take advantage of social media advertising programmes like Facebook Ads or Instagram's paid partnerships.
7. **Affiliate Marketing**: Promote products from other companies and earn a commission for each sale made through your referral links.
8. **Sponsored Posts**: Partner with brands to create sponsored content and earn money for promoting their products or services.
9. **Sell Your Own Products**: Launch and sell your own merchandise or digital products directly to your followers.
10. **Offer Services**: Use your platform to offer services such as coaching, consulting, or freelance work.
11. **Join Creator Funds**: Participate in creator fund programmes offered by platforms like TikTok and YouTube for additional income.
12. **Utilize Patreon or Subscriptions**: Offer exclusive content to subscribers who pay a monthly fee.
13. **Crowdfunding**: Use platforms like Kickstarter or GoFundMe to raise funds for specific projects or ventures.
14. **Leverage Analytics**: Use social media analytics tools to track your performance and optimize your content strategy.
15. **Run Contests and Giveaways**: Engage your audience and attract new followers by hosting contests and giveaways.
16. **Use SEO Techniques**: Optimize your profiles and content for search engines to increase discoverability.
17. **Create Viral Content**: Focus on creating shareable content that has the potential to go viral and attract a massive audience.
18. **Monetise Live Streams**: Use live streaming features to engage with your audience in real-time and receive tips or donations.
19. **Write Sponsored Blog Posts**: If you have a blog, write posts sponsored by brands to earn additional income.
20. **Attend Social Media Workshops**: Keep up-to-date with the latest trends and strategies by attending workshops and webinars.

Chapter 1
Create Quality Content

Creating quality content is the cornerstone of a successful social media presence. It is the primary way to engage your audience, attract new followers, and ultimately, monetise your social media channels. In this comprehensive guide, we will delve into the various aspects of producing high-quality, engaging content that resonates with your audience and sets you apart from the competition.

Understanding Your Audience

The first step in creating quality content is to understand your audience. Who are they? What are their interests, needs, and preferences? Conducting thorough audience research will provide you with valuable insights into the type of content that will appeal to them. Use analytics tools to gather data on your followers' demographics, behavior, and engagement patterns. Pay attention to the feedback they provide through comments, messages, and surveys. This information will help you tailor your content to meet their expectations and keep them coming back for more.

Setting Clear Goals

Before you start creating content, it is important to set clear goals. What do you want to achieve with your social media presence? Are you looking to increase brand awareness, drive traffic to your website, generate leads, or boost sales? Having a clear understanding of your objectives will guide your content creation process and ensure that every piece of content you produce serves a purpose. Your goals will also help you measure the success of your content and make necessary adjustments to improve your strategy.

Crafting a Content Strategy

A well-thought-out content strategy is essential for creating quality content consistently. Start by defining your content pillars – the main topics or themes that your content will revolve around. These should align with your brand's values and resonate with your audience. Next, create a content calendar to plan and organise your content in advance. This will help you maintain a consistent posting schedule and ensure that you cover all relevant topics. Additionally, a content calendar allows you to prepare for important events, holidays, and trends that you can leverage to engage your audience.

High-Quality Visuals

Visual content is a powerful tool for capturing your audience's attention and conveying your message effectively. Invest in high-quality visuals, including images, videos, and graphics, to make your content more appealing and professional. Use tools like Canva, Adobe Spark, or Photoshop to create eye-catching visuals that align with your brand's aesthetic. When it comes to videos, ensure they are well-produced, with clear audio and visuals. Remember, the quality of your visuals reflects the quality of your brand, so it is worth investing time and resources into getting them right.

Compelling Copy

While visuals are important, the copy that accompanies them is equally crucial. Your captions, headlines, and descriptions should be compelling, clear, and concise. Use a conversational tone to make your content more relatable and engaging. Incorporate storytelling techniques to create a connection with your audience and make your content more memorable. Additionally, use relevant keywords and hashtags to increase the discoverability of your content and attract new followers.

Engaging Formats

Diversifying your content formats can help you keep your audience engaged and cater to different preferences. Experiment with various formats, such as blog posts, infographics, videos, podcasts, and live streams. Each format offers unique benefits and can be used to convey different types of information. For example, videos are great for tutorials and behind-the-scenes content, while infographics are ideal for presenting data and statistics in a visually appealing way. By mixing up your content formats, you can keep your feed fresh and interesting, and cater to a wider range of audience preferences.

Authenticity and Transparency

In the age of social media, authenticity and transparency are highly valued by audiences. People want to connect with real, relatable individuals and brands. Be authentic in your content by sharing your true thoughts, experiences, and values. Don't be afraid to show the human side of your brand, including behind-the-scenes glimpses and personal stories. Additionally, be transparent about any sponsored content or partnerships to build trust with your audience. Authenticity and transparency will help you create a genuine connection with your followers and foster long-term loyalty.

Consistency

Consistency is key to building a strong social media presence. Posting regularly keeps your audience engaged and ensures that your content remains top of mind. However, consistency is not just about frequency; it also refers to the quality and style of your content. Maintain a consistent brand voice, aesthetic, and messaging across all your social media channels. This will help you create a cohesive and recognisable brand identity that your audience can easily identify and connect with.

Measuring Success

To ensure that your content is resonating with your audience and achieving your goals, it is important to measure its performance regularly. Use social media analytics tools to track key metrics such as engagement, reach, and conversions. Analyze which types of content perform best and identify any patterns or trends. Use this data to refine your content strategy and make informed decisions about future content. Regularly measuring and analyzing your content's performance will help you optimize your strategy and achieve better results.

Adapting and Evolving

The social media landscape is constantly changing, and it is important to stay updated with the latest trends and best practices. Keep an eye on emerging trends and be willing to experiment with new content formats and strategies. Follow industry leaders and competitors to see what is working for them and how you can apply similar tactics to your own content. Additionally, be open to feedback from your audience and use it to improve your content. Adapting and evolving your content strategy will help you stay relevant and continue to resonate with your audience over time.

Conclusion

Creating quality content is a continuous process that requires dedication, creativity, and strategic planning. By understanding your audience, setting clear goals, crafting a comprehensive content strategy, and focusing on high-quality visuals and compelling copy, you can produce engaging content that resonates with your audience. Consistency, authenticity, and regular performance measurement are key to maintaining a successful social media presence. Stay adaptable and open to new ideas, and you will be well on your way to maximizing your social media income through quality content.

Chapter 2
Utilize Multiple Platforms

Utilizing multiple social media platforms is a strategic approach to expanding your reach, engaging a broader audience, and maximizing your income potential. Each social media platform offers unique features, audience demographics, and content formats, making it essential to diversify your presence across several of them. This guide will provide an in-depth look at the benefits, strategies, and best practices for leveraging multiple platforms effectively.

Understanding the Benefits

1. **Wider Reach**: Different platforms attract different user bases. By diversifying, you can tap into various audience segments, increasing your overall reach.
2. **Platform-Specific Strengths**: Each platform has its strengths. Instagram is great for visual content, Twitter for real-time updates, LinkedIn for professional networking, and YouTube for long-form video content. Utilizing multiple platforms allows you to leverage these strengths.
3. **Risk Mitigation**: Relying on a single platform is risky. Changes in algorithms, policies, or even platform popularity can significantly impact your reach and income. Diversifying reduces this risk.
4. **Enhanced Engagement**: Different platforms offer various ways to engage with your audience. By using multiple platforms, you can interact with your followers in multiple ways, increasing overall engagement.
5. **Increased Monetisation Opportunities**: Each platform has its monetisation options, such as ads, sponsorships, and direct sales. By being active on multiple platforms, you can maximize these opportunities.

Choosing the Right Platforms

The first step in diversifying your social media presence is selecting the right platforms. Consider the following factors:

1. **Audience Demographics**: Research the user demographics of each platform to ensure they align with your target audience. For example, Instagram has a younger user base, while Facebook's user base is more diverse in age.
2. **Content Type**: Determine the type of content you will be creating. If you produce a lot of video content, YouTube and TikTok might be ideal. For written content, consider LinkedIn or a blog.
3. **Platform Features**: Evaluate the features of each platform and how they align with your content strategy. For instance, Instagram's Stories and Reels are great for short, engaging videos, while Pinterest is excellent for visual inspiration and tutorials.
4. **Competitor Analysis**: Look at where your competitors are active and how they engage their audience. This can provide insights into which platforms might work best for you.

Creating Platform - Specific Strategies

Each platform requires a tailored approach to maximize its potential. Here's how to create effective strategies for different platforms:

1. **Instagram**:
   - Focus on high-quality visual content such as photos, videos, and graphics.
   - Use Stories, Reels, and IGTV to engage with your audience in different ways.
   - Utilize hashtags and location tags to increase discoverability.
   - Collaborate with influencers and brands to expand your reach.
2. **Twitter**:
   - Share real-time updates, news, and trends.
   - Engage with followers through retweets, likes, and replies.
   - Use hashtags to join and start conversations.
   - Share links to your content on other platforms to drive traffic.
3. **Facebook**:
   - Create a mix of content types, including text, images, videos, and links.
   - Use Facebook Groups to build a community around your niche.
   - Leverage Facebook Ads to target specific demographics.
   - Host live events and webinars to engage with your audience in real-time.
4. **LinkedIn**:
   - Share professional and industry-related content.
   - Publish articles and thought leadership pieces to establish authority.
   - Network with professionals in your field.
   - Use LinkedIn Groups to connect with like-minded individuals.
5. **YouTube**:
   - Focus on high-quality, informative, and entertaining video content.
   - Optimize your video titles, descriptions, and tags for SEO.
   - Engage with your audience through comments and community posts.
   - Collaborate with other YouTubers to reach new audiences.

6. **Pinterest**:
   - Create visually appealing pins that link back to your website or blog.
   - Organize your pins into boards to make them easy to navigate.
   - Use keywords in your pin descriptions to improve search visibility.
   - Engage with other users by repinning and commenting on their content.
7. **TikTok**:
   - Produce short, engaging, and creative videos.
   - Participate in trending challenges and use popular sounds.
   - Engage with your audience through comments and duets.
   - Collaborate with other TikTok creators to expand your reach.

Managing Multiple Platforms

Managing multiple social media platforms can be challenging, but with the right tools and strategies, it becomes manageable. Here are some tips:

1. **Content Calendar**: Create a content calendar to plan and schedule your posts in advance. This ensures consistency and helps you stay organized.
2. **Social Media Management Tools**: Use tools like Hootsuite, Buffer, or Sprout Social to manage your accounts, schedule posts, and track analytics from a single dashboard.
3. **Repurpose Content**: Adapt and repurpose your content for different platforms. For example, a blog post can be turned into a series of tweets, an infographic, and a video.
4. **Automate Where Possible**: Automate repetitive tasks such as posting and reporting to save time and focus on content creation and engagement.
5. **Consistent Branding**: Maintain consistent branding across all platforms, including your profile picture, bio, and overall aesthetic. This helps create a cohesive and recognisable brand identity.
6. **Monitor Analytics**: Regularly review your performance analytics to understand what's working and what's not. Use this data to refine your strategies and improve your content.

Engaging with Your Audience

Engagement is crucial for building a loyal following across multiple platforms. Here's how to engage effectively:

1. **Respond to Comments and Messages**: Take the time to reply to comments and messages from your followers. This shows that you value their input and fosters a sense of community.
2. **Ask Questions and Solicit Feedback**: Encourage your audience to interact with your content by asking questions and seeking their feedback.
3. **Host Live Sessions**: Use live streaming features to interact with your audience in real-time. Answer their questions, share behind-the-scenes content, and discuss relevant topics.
4. **Run Contests and Giveaways**: Engage your audience by hosting contests and giveaways. This can increase your visibility and attract new followers.
5. **Feature User-Generated Content**: Showcase content created by your followers. This not only provides you with additional content but also makes your followers feel valued and appreciated.

Staying Updated with Trends

The social media landscape is constantly evolving, and staying updated with the latest trends and best practices is crucial. Follow industry blogs, attend webinars, and participate in online communities to keep abreast of new developments. Being adaptable and willing to experiment with new features and strategies will help you stay relevant and ahead of the competition.

Conclusion

Utilizing multiple social media platforms is an effective way to reach a broader audience, increase engagement, and maximise your income potential. By understanding the unique strengths of each platform and tailoring your strategies accordingly, you can create a diverse and robust social media presence. Remember to manage your platforms efficiently, engage with your audience regularly, and stay updated with the latest trends to achieve long-term success. Diversifying your social media presence is not just a smart strategy; it's a necessity in today's dynamic digital landscape.

Chapter 3
Engage with Your Followers

Engaging with your followers is a crucial aspect of building a loyal and active community on social media. Interaction fosters connection, trust, and loyalty, which can significantly enhance your online presence and impact. This guide will provide a comprehensive overview of effective engagement strategies, focusing on comments, messages, and live sessions.

Importance of Engagement

Engagement is more than just responding to comments or messages; it's about creating a two-way communication channel with your audience. This interaction makes followers feel valued and heard, fostering a sense of community and belonging. High engagement rates can also boost your visibility on social media algorithms, leading to increased reach and growth.

Responding to Comments

Responding to comments is one of the simplest yet most effective ways to engage with your audience. When followers take the time to comment on your posts, acknowledging their input shows appreciation and encourages further interaction.

1. **Timely Responses**: Aim to respond to comments promptly. Quick replies indicate that you are active and attentive, which can encourage more followers to engage.
2. **Personalised Replies**: Avoid generic responses. Personalise your replies to show that you genuinely care about each follower's input. Address them by their name and refer specifically to their comment.
3. **Encourage Conversations**: Use your responses to spark further dialogue. Ask follow-up questions or seek their opinions on related topics to keep the conversation going.
4. **Acknowledge Positive and Negative Feedback**: Appreciate compliments and constructive criticism alike. Responding to negative comments professionally and constructively can turn a dissatisfied follower into a loyal one.

Engaging Through Messages

Direct messages (DMs) offer a more private and personal way to interact with your followers. They are ideal for addressing specific concerns, providing detailed information, and building deeper connections.

1. **Be Accessible**: Make it clear that your DMs are open for questions, feedback, and conversation. Encourage followers to reach out to you.
2. **Personal Touch**: Personalize your messages to show that you're not sending automated replies. Mention their name and reference their query or comment directly.
3. **Provide Value**: Use DMs to offer exclusive content, personalized advice, or special offers. This can make followers feel valued and appreciated.
4. **Follow Up**: After resolving an issue or answering a question, follow up to ensure satisfaction. This shows that you care about their experience and fosters loyalty.

Hosting Live Sessions

Live sessions are a dynamic way to interact with your audience in real-time. They provide an opportunity for immediate feedback, authentic interaction, and enhanced connection.

1. **Plan Ahead**: Announce your live sessions in advance to give followers time to prepare. Choose a time that suits your audience's schedule.
2. **Engage During the Session**: Interact with viewers by addressing them by name, answering their questions, and acknowledging their comments. Make the session interactive by asking for their input and opinions.
3. **Provide Value**: Offer valuable content during your live sessions, such as tutorials, Q & A sessions, behind-the-scenes looks, or special announcements. This encourages more followers to join and participate.
4. **Follow Up Post-Session**: After the live session, thank participants and address any unanswered questions. Highlight key moments from the session in your posts to keep the engagement going.

Creating a Sense of Community

Building a loyal community involves more than just responding to comments and messages; it's about creating a space where followers feel connected and valued.

1. **Encourage User-Generated Content**: Invite followers to share their content related to your brand or niche. Feature their posts on your profile to show appreciation.
2. **Host Contests and Giveaways**: Engage followers by hosting contests and giveaways. This not only boosts interaction but also increases your reach.
3. **Showcase Testimonials and Success Stories**: Share positive feedback and success stories from your followers. This builds trust and shows that you value their achievements.

Conclusion

Engaging with your followers through comments, messages, and live sessions is essential for building a loyal and active community. Timely and personalized responses, valuable interactions, and creating a sense of community can significantly enhance your online presence. By prioritizing engagement, you not only foster loyalty but also drive growth and success on social media.

Chapter 4
Use Hashtags Strategically

Using hashtags strategically is a powerful method to enhance the visibility and reach of your content on social media platforms. Hashtags categorize your content, making it discoverable to a wider audience beyond your immediate followers. This guide will provide a comprehensive overview of the importance of hashtags, how to select the right ones, and best practices for using them effectively.

Importance of Hashtags

Hashtags serve as a bridge between your content and potential followers who are interested in similar topics. By tagging your posts with relevant hashtags, you can:

1. **Increase Discoverability**: Hashtags make your content searchable. Users who follow or search for specific hashtags can discover your posts, expanding your reach.
2. **Join Conversations**: Hashtags allow you to join larger conversations on trending topics, events, or themes, increasing the likelihood of your content being seen by a relevant audience.
3. **Enhance Engagement**: Posts with hashtags generally receive more engagement than those without. Hashtags can boost likes, comments, shares, and overall interaction.
4. **Build Community**: Using niche-specific hashtags can help you connect with a community of like-minded individuals, fostering a sense of belonging and loyalty.

Selecting the Right Hashtags

Choosing the right hashtags is crucial for maximizing their effectiveness. Here's how to select the best ones:

1. **Relevance**: Ensure that the hashtags you use are directly related to your content. Irrelevant hashtags can confuse users and reduce your credibility.
2. **Popularity**: While popular hashtags can increase visibility, they also come with high competition. Balance using popular hashtags with niche-specific ones to maximize reach and engagement.
3. **Specificity**: Use specific hashtags to target a more focused audience. Niche hashtags might have fewer posts, but they often attract a more engaged and relevant audience.
4. **Trends**: Stay updated with trending hashtags in your industry or niche. Leveraging current trends can boost your content's visibility and relevance.
5. **Branded Hashtags**: Create and use branded hashtags to promote your brand and encourage user-generated content. This helps in building brand identity and community.

Best Practices for Using Hashtags

To harness the full potential of hashtags, follow these best practices:

1. **Optimal Number of Hashtags**: Different platforms have varying recommendations for the number of hashtags. On Instagram, you can use up to 30 hashtags, but 5-10 well-chosen ones can be more effective. Twitter, with its character limit, is best suited for 1-2 hashtags. Experiment to find what works best for your audience.
2. **Placement**: On Instagram, hashtags can be placed in the caption or comments. For a cleaner look, many users prefer adding them in the first comment. On other platforms like Twitter and LinkedIn, include hashtags within the post itself.
3. **Mix of Hashtags**: Use a mix of popular, moderate, and niche-specific hashtags. This increases your chances of reaching different segments of your target audience.
4. **Research**: Use tools like Hashtagify, RiteTag, or the search function within platforms to research hashtags. These tools can provide insights into a hashtag's popularity, usage, and related tags.
5. **Consistency**: Regularly use hashtags in your posts to maintain and grow your visibility. However, avoid using the same set of hashtags for every post. Rotate and mix them to prevent appearing spammy and to reach different audiences.
6. **Evaluate Performance**: Track the performance of your hashtags using analytics tools. Assess which hashtags drive the most engagement and refine your strategy accordingly.

Avoiding Hashtag Pitfalls

While hashtags are beneficial, misusing them can have negative effects. Here are some pitfalls to avoid:

1. **Overuse**: Using too many hashtags, especially irrelevant ones, can make your posts look cluttered and spammy.
2. **Banned Hashtags**: Some hashtags are banned by platforms due to misuse or inappropriate content. Using them can shadowban your posts, reducing visibility.
3. **Generic Hashtags**: Extremely generic hashtags like #Love or #Fun is highly competitive and may not significantly boost your reach. Aim for a balance between generic and specific hashtags.

Conclusion

Using hashtags strategically is a key tactic for increasing your content's visibility and reach on social media. By selecting relevant, popular, and niche-specific hashtags, and following best practices for their use, you can enhance your engagement and connect with a broader audience. Regularly evaluate your hashtag performance and stay updated with trends to continuously refine your strategy. Effective hashtag use can significantly amplify your social media presence and contribute to your overall success.

Chapter 5
Collaborate with Influencers

Collaborating with influencers is a powerful strategy to expand your reach, gain new followers, and enhance your social media presence. Influencers, with their established follower bases and credibility, can help you tap into new audiences and boost your brand visibility. Here's a comprehensive summary of the benefits, strategies, and best practices for successful influencer collaborations.

Benefits of Collaborating with Influencers

1. **Expanded Reach**: Influencers have dedicated followers who trust their recommendations. Partnering with them allows you to access and engage with their audience, significantly expanding your reach.
2. **Increased Credibility**: When an influencer endorses your brand, their followers view it as a trusted recommendation. This can enhance your brand's credibility and attract new followers.
3. **Targeted Audience**: Influencers often have niche audiences. Collaborating with influencers in your niche ensures that your content reaches a highly relevant and engaged audience.
4. **Content Creation**: Influencers are skilled content creators. Collaborating with them can result in high-quality, creative content that you can share on your platforms.

Strategies for Effective Influencer Collaborations

1. **Identify the Right Influencers**: Choose influencers whose audience aligns with your target market. Consider factors such as their niche, engagement rates, and the authenticity of their interactions with followers.

2. **Build Relationships**: Establish genuine relationships with influencers before proposing collaborations. Engage with their content, comment on their posts, and share their work to build rapport.
3. **Define Clear Objectives**: Clearly outline what you aim to achieve with the collaboration. Whether it's increasing brand awareness, driving sales, or growing your follower base, having clear objectives will guide the partnership.
4. **Offer Value**: Ensure the collaboration is mutually beneficial. Offer influencers something of value, whether it's payment, free products, or exclusive access to your services.
5. **Create Authentic Content**: Allow influencers the creative freedom to produce content that resonates with their audience. Authenticity is key to successful influencer marketing.

Best Practices for Collaborating with Influencers

1. **Transparent Communication**: Be clear about your expectations, deliverables, and timelines. Open and honest communication ensures a smooth collaboration.
2. **Contractual Agreements**: Have a formal agreement outlining the terms of the collaboration, including content guidelines, posting schedules, and compensation. This protects both parties and ensures clarity.
3. **Leverage Multiple Platforms**: Encourage influencers to share content across various platforms for maximum exposure. Cross-platform promotions can amplify your reach.
4. **Monitor and Measure**: Track the performance of the collaboration using analytics tools. Measure key metrics such as engagement, follower growth, and conversion rates to evaluate the success of the partnership.
5. **Acknowledge and Engage**: Show appreciation for the influencer's work by acknowledging their efforts publicly. Engage with the content they create for you by liking, sharing, and commenting.

Conclusion

Partnering with influencers is a strategic way to expand your reach, gain new followers, and enhance your brand's credibility. By carefully selecting the right influencers, building genuine relationships, and creating authentic, valuable content, you can leverage influencer collaborations to achieve your social media goals. Transparent communication, contractual agreements, and performance tracking are essential for successful partnerships. Embrace the power of influencer marketing to elevate your social media presence and connect with a broader, more engaged audience.

Chapter 6
Monetise with Ads

Monetizing ads on social media platforms is a highly effective strategy for generating income and expanding your reach. Social media advertising programmes like Facebook Ads and Instagram's paid partnerships offer robust tools and features that allow you to target specific audiences, increase brand awareness, and drive conversions. Here's a comprehensive summary of how to effectively monetise with ads on social media.

Benefits of Social Media Advertising

1. **Targeted Advertising**: Social media platforms offer advanced targeting options, allowing you to reach specific demographics, interests, and behaviors. This ensures that your ads are seen by a relevant audience.
2. **Increased Visibility**: Paid ads enhance your visibility on social media, placing your content in front of users who may not follow you yet. This can lead to increased brand awareness and follower growth.
3. **Measurable Results**: Advertising programmes provide detailed analytics and performance metrics. You can track the success of your ads in real-time and make data-driven decisions to optimize your campaigns.
4. **Cost-Effective**: Social media ads can be cost-effective, offering various budgeting options to suit different financial capacities. You can set daily or lifetime budgets and adjust your spend based on performance.

Setting Up Social Media Ads

1. **Define Your Goals**: Before creating ads, clearly define your objectives. Common goals include increasing website traffic,

generating leads, boosting sales, or growing your social media following.

2. **Choose the Right Platform**: Select the social media platform that best aligns with your target audience. Facebook, Instagram, Twitter, LinkedIn, and Pinterest each offer unique ad formats and targeting options.
3. **Create Engaging Content**: Develop high-quality, engaging ad content that resonates with your audience. Use compelling visuals, strong calls-to-action, and concise messaging to capture attention.
4. **Set a Budget**: Determine your budget based on your goals and resources. Platforms offer flexible budgeting options, allowing you to control your ad spend effectively.

Best Practices for Social Media Advertising

1. **Audience Targeting**: Utilize the advanced targeting options available to reach a specific audience. Define your audience based on demographics, interests, behaviors, and even custom data such as email lists.
2. **A/B Testing**: Run A/B tests on your ads to compare different versions and identify which performs best. Test variables like ad copy, images, and targeting to optimize your campaigns.
3. **Optimize for Mobile**: Ensure your ads are mobile-friendly, as a significant portion of social media users access these platforms on their mobile devices. Use vertical or square formats and clear, legible text.
4. **Monitor and Adjust**: Regularly monitor your ad performance using the analytics tools provided by the platforms. Adjust your targeting, budget, and content based on the insights gained to improve results.
5. **Utilize Retargeting**: Implement retargeting strategies to reach users who have previously interacted with your brand. This can help convert potential customers who have shown interest but have not yet taken action.

Monetising Through Paid Partnerships

In addition to direct advertising, you can monetise your social media presence through paid partnerships. Platforms like Instagram facilitate collaborations between influencers and brands, allowing you to earn money by promoting products or services.

1. **Build a Strong Profile**: Establish a strong, authentic profile with a dedicated follower base. Brands are more likely to partner with influencers who have a genuine and engaged audience.
2. **Collaborate with Brands**: Reach out to brands or use platforms that connect influencers with companies looking for partnership opportunities. Ensure that the brands align with your niche and audience.
3. **Transparent Disclosure**: Always disclose paid partnerships clearly to maintain transparency and trust with your audience. Use appropriate tags and hashtags like #ad or #sponsored.

Conclusion

Monetizing ads on social media is a powerful way to generate income and expand your reach. By leveraging the advanced targeting options, creating engaging content, and using data-driven strategies, you can optimize your ad campaigns for maximum effectiveness. Additionally, exploring paid partnerships can provide a lucrative revenue stream, further enhancing your social media monetisation efforts. Embrace these strategies to elevate your brand and achieve your financial goals on social media.

Chapter 7
Affiliate Marketing

Affiliate marketing is a popular and effective strategy for monetising your online presence by promoting products from other companies and earning a commission for each sale made through your referral links. This method allows you to leverage your influence and audience to generate income without the need to create your own products. Here's a comprehensive summary of how to effectively engage in affiliate marketing.

Understanding Affiliate Marketing

Affiliate marketing involves partnering with companies to promote their products or services. As an affiliate marketer, you receive a unique referral link or code to share with your audience. When someone uses your link to make a purchase, you earn a commission. This arrangement benefits all parties: the company gains sales, the customer discovers recommended products, and you earn a commission.

Benefits of Affiliate Marketing

1. **Low Risk and Cost**: Affiliate marketing requires minimal upfront investment. You don't need to create products, manage inventory, or handle customer service. Your primary task is to promote existing products.
2. **Passive Income**: Once your affiliate links are placed in content such as blog posts, social media, or videos, they can generate income continuously without ongoing effort.
3. **Flexibility**: You can promote a wide range of products from different companies, allowing you to choose items that align with your niche and audience.
4. **Scalability**: As your audience grows, your potential earnings from affiliate marketing can increase proportionally. High-traffic platforms can significantly boost your commissions.

Choosing the Right Affiliate Programmes

1. **Relevance**: Select products and services that are relevant to your niche and audience. Promoting items that align with your content ensures higher engagement and trust.
2. **Reputable Companies**: Partner with reputable companies that offer high-quality products and have positive reviews. This maintains your credibility with your audience.
3. **Commission Rates**: Compare commission rates among different programmes. Higher rates can lead to more substantial earnings, but also consider the product's price and conversion rate.
4. **Support and Resources**: Look for programmes that provide marketing materials, training, and support. These resources can help you effectively promote their products.

Effective Promotion Strategies

1. **Content Creation**: Create valuable and informative content that naturally incorporates your affiliate links. Blog posts, product reviews, tutorials, and comparison articles are effective formats.

2. **Social Media**: Use social media platforms to share your affiliate links. Engage your followers with compelling posts, stories, and videos that highlight the benefits of the products.
3. **Email Marketing**: Build an email list and send newsletters featuring your affiliate products. Personal recommendations and exclusive offers can encourage subscribers to make purchases.
4. **SEO Optimisation**: Optimise your content for search engines to attract organic traffic. Use relevant keywords and provide comprehensive information to rank higher in search results.
5. **Transparency**: Always disclose your affiliate relationships. Transparency builds trust with your audience and complies with legal regulations.

Tracking and Optimising Performance

1. **Analytics Tools**: Use analytics tools provided by affiliate programmes to track clicks, conversions, and commissions. This data helps you understand what works and what doesn't.
2. **A/B Testing**: Experiment with different promotional strategies, content formats, and calls-to-action. A/B testing allows you to identify the most effective approaches.
3. **Audience Feedback**: Pay attention to feedback from your audience. If certain products resonate more, focus your efforts on promoting similar items.
4. **Continuous Improvement**: Regularly update your content and strategies based on performance data and market trends. Staying current ensures ongoing success in affiliate marketing.

Best Practices for Affiliate Marketing

1. **Authenticity**: Promote products you genuinely believe in and have personally used or thoroughly researched. Authenticity enhances trust and credibility.
2. **Balanced Promotion**: Avoid overwhelming your audience with constant promotions. Balance affiliate content with other valuable, non-promotional content.
3. **Legal Compliance**: Ensure your affiliate marketing activities comply with legal regulations, including clear disclosures and adherence to platform policies.

Conclusion

Affiliate marketing is a powerful way to monetise your online presence by promoting products from other companies and earning commissions on sales. By selecting the right affiliate programmes, creating engaging content, and using effective promotional strategies, you can generate a steady stream of income. Tracking and optimizing your performance, maintaining authenticity, and balancing promotional content will further enhance your success in affiliate marketing. This approach not only provides financial benefits but also adds value to your audience by introducing them to quality products and services.

Chapter 8
Sponsored Posts

Sponsored posts are a lucrative method for monetising your social media presence by partnering with brands to promote their products or services. This form of advertising allows you to create content that aligns with your brand while earning money for your promotional efforts. Here's a comprehensive summary of how to effectively engage in creating sponsored posts.

Understanding Sponsored Posts

Sponsored posts are content created by influencers or social media users on behalf of a brand. In exchange for promoting the brand's products or services, you receive compensation. These posts can appear in various formats, such as images, videos, blog entries, or social media updates, and are designed to reach the influencer's audience authentically.

Benefits of Sponsored Posts

1. **Monetisation**: Sponsored posts offer a direct way to earn money by leveraging your social media influence.
2. **Brand Relationships**: Collaborating with brands can lead to long-term partnerships, opening up more opportunities for future collaborations.
3. **Content Variety**: Sponsored posts can diversify your content, providing fresh material for your audience while maintaining relevance to your niche.

4. **Audience Engagement**: If done correctly, sponsored content can engage your audience and provide them with valuable product recommendations.

Selecting the Right Brands

1. **Relevance**: Choose brands that align with your niche and audience's interests. The more relevant the product, the more authentic and effective the promotion will be.
2. **Reputation**: Partner with reputable brands that offer high-quality products. Your credibility is tied to the brands you endorse.
3. **Values Alignment**: Ensure that the brand's values match yours. Authentic partnerships are more likely to resonate with your audience.

Creating Effective Sponsored Content

1. **Authenticity**: Create genuine content that naturally integrates the brand's products or services. Authentic endorsements are more likely to engage your audience and lead to conversions.
2. **Transparency**: Always disclose sponsored posts clearly to maintain trust with your audience. Use hashtags like #ad or #sponsored to comply with advertising regulations.
3. **Quality**: Produce high-quality content that meets both your standards and the brand's expectations. Invest time in creating visually appealing and informative posts.
4. **Engagement**: Encourage interaction by asking questions, seeking opinions, or offering exclusive deals related to the sponsored product.

Negotiating and Managing Partnerships

1. **Compensation**: Negotiate fair compensation based on your reach, engagement rates, and the scope of the project. Be clear about your rates and deliverables.
2. **Contractual Agreements**: Have a formal agreement outlining the terms of the partnership, including deadlines, content guidelines, and payment details.
3. **Communication**: Maintain open and regular communication with the brand. Understand their expectations and provide updates on the content creation process.

Measuring Success

1. **Analytics**: Use analytics tools to track the performance of your sponsored posts. Measure metrics such as engagement rates, reach, and conversions to evaluate success.
2. **Feedback**: Seek feedback from both the brand and your audience. Positive feedback can lead to repeat collaborations, while constructive criticism can help you improve future sponsored content.

Conclusion

Sponsored posts are an effective way to monetise your social media presence by partnering with brands to promote their products or services. By selecting the right brands, creating authentic and high-quality content, and maintaining transparency and open communication, you can successfully engage in sponsored partnerships. This approach not only provides financial benefits but also enhances your content variety and strengthens your relationship with your audience.

Chapter 9
Sell Your Own Products

Selling your own products is a compelling way to monetise your social media presence and establish a direct revenue stream. Whether it's merchandise, digital products, or services, this approach allows you to leverage your influence and create a closer connection with your followers. Here's a comprehensive summary of how to effectively launch and sell your own products.

Benefits of Selling Your Own Products

1. **Revenue Generation**: Direct sales of your products can provide a significant income stream, reducing reliance on third-party advertising or sponsorships.
2. **Brand Identity**: Creating your own products helps strengthen your brand identity and presence. It reinforces your niche and builds a stronger connection with your audience.

3. **Control**: You have complete control over the product quality, pricing, and marketing strategies, allowing you to tailor everything to your brand's ethos and your audience's preferences.
4. **Customer Loyalty**: Selling products directly to your followers can enhance loyalty, as they feel more connected to your brand and its offerings.

Types of Products to Sell

1. **Merchandise**: Branded items such as clothing, accessories, and home goods. These products allow your followers to showcase their support and connection to your brand.
2. **Digital Products**: E-books, courses, printables, and digital art. Digital products often have lower production costs and can be delivered instantly, providing a convenient option for both you and your customers.
3. **Services**: Consulting, coaching, or personalized experiences. Offering services allows you to share your expertise and provide value directly to your followers.

Steps to Launch and Sell Your Products

1. **Market Research**: Understand your audience's needs and preferences. Conduct surveys, polls, or analyze engagement metrics to identify what products would resonate most with your followers.
2. **Product Development**: Develop high-quality products that align with your brand and audience's expectations. For physical merchandise, consider partnering with reputable manufacturers. For digital products, focus on creating valuable and well-designed content.
3. **Branding and Packaging**: Invest in professional branding and attractive packaging. Consistent and appealing branding enhances perceived value and helps differentiate your products from competitors.
4. **Pricing Strategy**: Set competitive prices that reflect the quality and value of your products. Consider your costs, market rates, and your audience's willingness to pay.

Marketing Your Products

1. **Content Marketing**: Use your social media platforms to create engaging content around your products. Share behind-the-scenes

looks, product demos, and user testimonials to generate interest and excitement.
2. **Influencer Partnerships**: Collaborate with other influencers to promote your products. This can expand your reach and introduce your offerings to new audiences.
3. **Email Marketing**: Build an email list and send regular updates, exclusive offers, and product launches to your subscribers. Personalized emails can drive engagement and sales.
4. **Promotional Campaigns**: Run special promotions, discounts, or limited-time offers to create urgency and boost sales. Seasonal sales or holiday promotions can be particularly effective.

Sales Platforms and Logistics

1. **E-commerce Platforms**: Set up an online store using platforms like Shopify, WooCommerce, or Etsy. These platforms offer user-friendly tools to manage inventory, process payments, and track orders.
2. **Social Media Shops**: Utilize social media features like Instagram Shopping, Facebook Shops, and Pinterest Buyable Pins to sell directly through your social media profiles.
3. **Order Fulfillment**: Plan for efficient order fulfillment and shipping. For physical products, consider using fulfillment services that can handle storage, packing, and shipping. For digital products, automate delivery to ensure instant access for your customers.
4. **Customer Service**: Provide excellent customer service to build trust and encourage repeat business. Respond promptly to inquiries, address issues professionally, and maintain open communication with your customers.

Measuring Success

1. **Sales Metrics**: Track key metrics such as total sales, conversion rates, and average order value. Use this data to assess the success of your product launches and marketing strategies.
2. **Customer Feedback**: Collect feedback from your customers to understand their experiences and identify areas for improvement. Positive reviews can be used as testimonials, while constructive criticism can guide product enhancements.
3. **Social Media Analytics**: Monitor engagement metrics on your promotional posts to gauge interest and adjust your content strategy accordingly.

Conclusion

Selling your own products is a powerful way to monetise your social media presence while building a stronger connection with your audience. By conducting thorough market research, developing high-quality products, and implementing effective marketing strategies, you can successfully launch and sell merchandise or digital products. Leveraging e-commerce platforms and social media shops can streamline the sales process, while providing excellent customer service can enhance loyalty and encourage repeat business. This approach not only generates revenue but also reinforces your brand identity and fosters a deeper relationship with your followers.

Chapter 10
Offer Services

Offering services such as coaching, consulting, or freelance work through your social media platform is an excellent way to monetise your expertise and build deeper connections with your audience. This strategy leverages your skills and knowledge to provide value directly to your followers, generating income while enhancing your brand's credibility. Here's a comprehensive summary of how to effectively offer services through your social media presence.

Benefits of Offering Services

1. **Direct Revenue**: Offering services can be a significant source of income. As these are often high-value offerings, they can provide a substantial return for your time and expertise.
2. **Enhanced Credibility**: Providing services showcases your expertise and builds your reputation as an authority in your field. This can attract more followers and potential clients.
3. **Personal Connection**: Services like coaching or consulting allow for one-on-one interactions, fostering stronger relationships with your audience.
4. **Flexibility and Control**: You can set your own schedule, choose your clients, and tailor your services to fit your strengths and interests.

Types of Services to Offer

1. **Coaching**: Offer personalized coaching sessions in areas such as fitness, life skills, business, or personal development. Tailored advice and guidance can help clients achieve their goals.
2. **Consulting**: Provide expert advice to businesses or individuals in your area of expertise, such as marketing, social media strategy, or financial planning.
3. **Freelance Work**: Offer your skills on a project basis. This could include writing, graphic design, web development, photography, or any other specialized service.

Steps to Offering Services

1. **Identify Your Niche**: Clearly define the services you will offer based on your expertise and your audience's needs. Ensure there is demand for the services you plan to provide.
2. **Create a Service Menu**: Develop a detailed list of your services, including descriptions, pricing, and any packages or special offers. Make this information easily accessible on your social media profiles and website.
3. **Promote Your Services**: Use your social media platforms to regularly promote your services. Share testimonials, case studies, and success stories to demonstrate the value you provide.
4. **Leverage Content**: Create content that highlights your expertise. This can include blog posts, videos, webinars, or live sessions that offer valuable insights and subtly promote your services.

Marketing and Engagement

1. **Content Marketing**: Share informative and engaging content that showcases your knowledge and skills. This can attract potential clients who are interested in your services.
2. **Social Proof**: Collect and share testimonials from satisfied clients. Positive reviews and word-of-mouth recommendations can significantly boost your credibility.
3. **Networking**: Engage with your audience and other professionals in your field. Networking can lead to referrals and new client opportunities.

4. **Offer Free Samples**: Provide free consultations or limited-time offers to attract potential clients. This can give them a taste of your expertise and encourage them to book paid services.

Managing Your Services

1. **Booking System**: Implement a reliable booking system to manage appointments and streamline the scheduling process. Tools like Calendly or Acuity Scheduling can help.
2. **Client Communication**: Maintain clear and professional communication with your clients. Set expectations, provide regular updates, and be responsive to inquiries.
3. **Continuous Improvement**: Seek feedback from clients to improve your services. Regularly update your skills and stay informed about industry trends to provide the best possible service.

Conclusion

Offering services such as coaching, consulting, or freelance work through your social media platform is a powerful way to monetise your expertise and build stronger relationships with your audience. By identifying your niche, promoting your services effectively, and maintaining professional client management, you can create a successful service-based business. This approach not only generates direct revenue but also enhances your brand's credibility and fosters a loyal and engaged community.

Chapter 11
Join Creator Funds

Joining creator fund programmes offered by platforms like TikTok and YouTube is an excellent way to generate additional income from your social media activities. These programmes reward content creators based on their performance, engagement, and reach. Here's a comprehensive summary of how to effectively participate in creator fund programmes.

Understanding Creator Funds

Creator funds are monetary pools established by social media platforms to compensate content creators for their contributions. TikTok's Creator Fund and YouTube's Partner Programme are prominent examples, designed to support and incentivise creators by sharing a portion of the platforms' ad revenue.

Benefits of Joining Creator Funds

1. **Additional Income**: Creator funds provide a steady source of income based on the performance of your content. The more views and engagement your content receives, the higher your earnings.
2. **Recognition and Support**: Joining a creator fund can offer validation and recognition from the platform, boosting your credibility.
3. **Platform Features**: Participation often grants access to additional tools, features, and resources designed to help you enhance your content and grow your audience.

Eligibility and Requirements

1. **Content Quality**: Maintain high-quality, engaging content that adheres to the platform's community guidelines.
2. **Follower Count**: Platforms typically require a minimum number of followers or subscribers to join their creator fund programmes.
3. **Consistent Activity**: Regularly post content to keep your audience engaged and maintain your eligibility for the programme.
4. **Geographic Availability**: Creator funds are often available only in certain regions, so check the availability based on your location.

Steps to Join Creator Funds

1. **Meet the Requirements**: Ensure you meet the platform's eligibility criteria regarding followers, content quality, and engagement.
2. **Apply for the Programme**: Follow the application process outlined by the platform. This may involve signing up through your account settings and agreeing to the terms and conditions.
3. **Track Performance**: Use analytics tools provided by the platform to monitor your content's performance. Higher engagement and views translate to higher earnings.

Maximizing Your Earnings

1. **Engage with Your Audience**: Foster a loyal community by interacting with your followers through comments, live sessions, and direct messages.
2. **Create Viral Content**: Focus on creating content that is likely to be shared widely to maximize views and engagement.
3. **Stay Informed**: Keep up-to-date with platform updates and algorithm changes to optimise your content strategy.

Conclusion

Joining creator fund programmes on platforms like TikTok and YouTube is a valuable way to monetise your content and receive recognition for your work. By meeting eligibility requirements, applying for the programme, and consistently producing high-quality, engaging content, you can maximize your earnings and benefit from additional support and resources offered by the platforms. This approach not only provides financial rewards but also enhances your presence and influence on social media.

Chapter 12
Utilize Patreon or Subscriptions

Utilizing platforms like Patreon or subscription models on social media offers a powerful way to monetise your content by providing exclusive material to subscribers who pay a monthly fee. This approach helps generate a steady income stream and fosters a deeper connection with your most dedicated followers. Here's a comprehensive summary of how to effectively use Patreon or subscription models.

Understanding Patreon and Subscription Models

Patreon and similar platforms allow creators to offer exclusive content to their audience in exchange for a subscription fee. Followers, known as patrons or subscribers, pay a monthly fee to access this premium content, which can include behind-the-scenes updates, early access to new material, personalized content, or other exclusive benefits.

Benefits of Patreon and Subscriptions

1. **Steady Income**: Subscriptions provide a predictable monthly revenue stream, which can be more stable than ad-based income.
2. **Closer Community**: Offering exclusive content helps build a stronger, more engaged community. Subscribers feel valued and are more likely to support your work consistently.
3. **Creative Freedom**: With a direct income from your audience, you have greater creative freedom to produce content that truly resonates with your supporters, without relying on external advertisers.

Types of Exclusive Content

1. **Early Access**: Allow subscribers to view content before it is released to the general public.
2. **Exclusive Videos or Posts**: Create content that is only available to your subscribers, such as behind-the-scenes footage, tutorials, or in-depth articles.
3. **Live Streams and Q&A Sessions**: Host live events exclusively for your subscribers, providing them with direct interaction and engagement.
4. **Personalized Content**: Offer personalized messages, shoutouts, or customized content tailored to individual subscribers.

Setting Up and Promoting Your Patreon or Subscriptions

1. **Create Tiers**: Develop different subscription tiers with varying levels of access and benefits. Higher tiers should offer more exclusive content and perks.
2. **Promote Your Offer**: Use your social media platforms to promote your Patreon or subscription service. Explain the benefits of subscribing and highlight the value of the exclusive content you offer.
3. **Engage Your Audience**: Encourage your followers to join by creating compelling promotional content, such as teaser videos or behind-the-scenes glimpses of what subscribers can expect.

Maintaining Subscriber Satisfaction

1. **Consistent Content Delivery**: Regularly update your Patreon or subscription platform with new content to keep your subscribers engaged and satisfied.

2. **Interact with Subscribers**: Engage with your subscribers by responding to comments, messages, and feedback. Personal interaction can increase loyalty and retention.
3. **Seek Feedback**: Regularly ask for feedback from your subscribers to understand their preferences and improve your content offerings.

Maximizing Your Earnings

1. **Special Promotions**: Offer limited-time discounts or special promotions to attract new subscribers.
2. **Collaboration and Cross-Promotion**: Partner with other creators to cross-promote each other's subscription services, reaching new audiences.
3. **Transparency**: Be transparent about your goals and how subscriber funds are used. This builds trust and encourages continued support.

Conclusion

Utilizing Patreon or subscription models is an effective way to monetise your content by offering exclusive material to paying subscribers. By creating valuable and engaging content, promoting your subscription service effectively, and maintaining strong engagement with your subscribers, you can generate a steady income stream and build a loyal, supportive community. This approach not only provides financial stability but also fosters a deeper connection with your audience, allowing you to focus on creating content that truly resonates with your most dedicated followers.

Chapter 13
Crowdfunding

Crowdfunding is an innovative and effective way to raise funds for specific projects or ventures by appealing directly to your audience and the public. Platforms like Kickstarter and GoFundMe facilitate this process, allowing creators to gather financial support for their ideas. Here's a comprehensive summary of how to effectively utilise crowdfunding for your projects.

Understanding Crowdfunding

Crowdfunding involves soliciting small contributions from a large number of people, typically via the internet. Platforms like Kickstarter and GoFundMe provide a structured way to present your project, set funding goals, and collect donations. Contributors, often called backers, can support projects they believe in, usually in exchange for rewards or simply out of a desire to see the project succeed.

Benefits of Crowdfunding

1. **Access to Capital**: Crowdfunding allows you to raise significant amounts of money without relying on traditional financing methods like loans or investors.
2. **Market Validation**: Successfully funding a project through crowdfunding demonstrates public interest and market demand, validating your idea.
3. **Community Building**: Engaging with backers through crowdfunding builds a community around your project, fostering loyalty and support.
4. **Creative Freedom**: With funding from backers who believe in your vision, you maintain creative control over your project.

Choosing the Right Platform

1. **Kickstarter**: Ideal for creative projects such as films, games, and products. It operates on an all-or-nothing funding model, meaning you must reach your funding goal to receive any money.
2. **GoFundMe**: Suitable for personal causes, charitable projects, and ventures that might not fit into Kickstarter's creative categories. It allows you to keep whatever money you raise, regardless of whether you meet your goal.

Setting Up Your Campaign

1. **Define Your Goal**: Clearly outline what you aim to achieve with your project and how much money you need. Be realistic and transparent about the costs involved.
2. **Create a Compelling Story**: Craft a compelling narrative that explains why your project is important, how it will be executed, and why backers should care.
3. **Offer Attractive Rewards**: On platforms like Kickstarter, offer rewards or incentives for different levels of contribution. These can

range from thank-you notes and exclusive updates to products and experiences related to your project.

4. **Professional Presentation**: Invest time in creating high-quality visuals, including images and videos, to present your project professionally and attractively.

Promoting Your Campaign

1. **Leverage Social Media**: Use your social media platforms to spread the word about your campaign. Regular updates, engaging posts, and calls to action can drive traffic to your crowdfunding page.
2. **Engage Your Network**: Reach out to friends, family, and existing followers to gain initial support and momentum. Personal endorsements can significantly boost credibility.
3. **Media and PR**: Contact relevant media outlets, bloggers, and influencers who might be interested in covering your campaign. Press coverage can expand your reach considerably.

Managing Your Campaign

1. **Regular Updates**: Keep your backers informed with regular updates on the progress of your campaign and the project itself. Transparency builds trust and encourages continued support.
2. **Respond to Backers**: Engage with your backers by responding to their comments and messages promptly. This interaction shows appreciation and fosters a sense of community.

Conclusion

Crowdfunding on platforms like Kickstarter and GoFundMe is a powerful way to raise funds for specific projects or ventures. By setting a clear goal, crafting a compelling story, offering attractive rewards, and actively promoting your campaign, you can gather the financial support needed to bring your project to life. This approach not only provides the necessary funds but also builds a loyal community around your project, ensuring its success and sustainability.

Chapter 14

Leverage Analytics

Leverage Analytics:

Using social media analytics tools is crucial for tracking performance and optimizing your content strategy. Analytics provide insights into which types of content resonate most with your audience, helping you understand engagement patterns and demographic information. Key metrics include likes, shares, comments, and follower growth, as well as more detailed data like reach, impressions, and click-through rates. Tools such as Google Analytics, Facebook Insights, and Twitter Analytics offer comprehensive reports that can guide your content planning. By regularly reviewing these metrics, you can identify successful content, the best times to post, and the platforms where your audience is most active. This data-driven approach enables you to refine your strategy, enhance engagement, and ultimately grow your social media presence more effectively.

Run Contests and Giveaways:

Hosting contests and giveaways is an effective way to engage your audience and attract new followers. These events create excitement and encourage interaction, making your social media platforms more dynamic and lively. Contests can be simple, like asking followers to share a post or tag friends, or more complex, like creating user-generated content around a specific theme. Giveaways, where followers enter to win a prize, can increase visibility and attract new followers quickly. To maximize impact, ensure the rules are clear, the prizes are appealing, and the contest or giveaway is promoted across all your social media channels. Additionally, collaborating with other influencers or brands can expand reach and attract a broader audience. By running regular contests and giveaways, you can boost engagement, increase your follower count, and create a more interactive community around your brand.

Chapter 15
Run Contests and Giveaways

Running contests and giveaways is a highly effective strategy to engage your audience and attract new followers on social media. These activities generate excitement, foster interaction, and significantly increase your visibility, making your platforms more vibrant and appealing.

Benefits of Contests and Giveaways

1. **Increased Engagement**: Contests and giveaways encourage followers to interact with your content through likes, shares, comments, and tags. This heightened activity can boost your posts' visibility in social media algorithms.
2. **Follower Growth**: Offering attractive prizes incentivises people to follow your account and share your content, helping you reach a broader audience.
3. **Brand Awareness**: These events can introduce your brand to new potential followers, enhancing your visibility and reach.
4. **Community Building**: Contests and giveaways create a sense of community and loyalty among your followers, making them feel valued and more connected to your brand.

Planning and Executing Contests and Giveaways

1. **Define Clear Goals**: Determine what you aim to achieve with your contest or giveaway. Common goals include increasing followers, boosting engagement, or promoting a new product.
2. **Choose Appealing Prizes**: Select prizes that are relevant and appealing to your target audience. The more desirable the prize, the more likely people will participate and share your content.
3. **Set Simple Rules**: Ensure the rules are easy to understand and participate in. Common requirements include following your account, liking and sharing a post, tagging friends, or using a specific hashtag.
4. **Promote the Event**: Use all your social media channels to promote the contest or giveaway. Eye-catching visuals and compelling calls to action can help maximise participation. Collaborate with other influencers or brands to further expand your reach.
5. **Engage During the Event**: Keep the momentum going by interacting with participants, responding to comments, and sharing user-generated content related to the contest.
6. **Announce Winners Transparently**: Announce the winners publicly to maintain transparency and trust. Celebrate their win with a dedicated post and encourage them to share their excitement.

Post-Contest Follow-Up

1. **Thank Participants**: Show appreciation to everyone who participated. A thank-you post or a small incentive for all participants can foster goodwill.
2. **Analyze Results**: Review the contest's performance to understand what worked well and what could be improved. Metrics to consider include engagement rates, follower growth, and overall reach.

Conclusion

Running contests and giveaways is a powerful way to engage your audience and attract new followers. By carefully planning and executing these events, you can boost engagement, increase brand awareness, and build a loyal, interactive community around your social media presence. This approach not only enhances your visibility but also strengthens the connection between your brand and its followers.

Chapter 16
Use SEO Techniques

Using SEO (Search Engine Optimisation) techniques to optimize your social media profiles and content can significantly enhance your discoverability, driving more organic traffic to your platforms. Here's a comprehensive summary of how to effectively implement SEO strategies for your social media presence.

Benefits of SEO for Social Media

1. **Increased Visibility**: Optimised content ranks higher in search engine results, making it easier for potential followers to find you.
2. **Enhanced Engagement**: Higher visibility leads to more interactions, boosting your engagement rates.
3. **Brand Credibility**: Appearing in top search results increases your brand's credibility and authority.

Key SEO Techniques

1. **Keyword Research**: Identify relevant keywords and phrases that your target audience is likely to search for. Tools like Google Keyword Planner, Ahrefs, or SEMrush can help you find effective keywords.
2. **Optimize Profiles**: Include primary keywords in your profile descriptions, usernames, and bio sections. Ensure your profile information is complete, including links to your website and other social media accounts.
3. **Content Optimisation**: Incorporate keywords naturally into your posts, captions, and hashtags. Use variations of keywords to cover different search terms. Include keywords in image alt texts and video descriptions to enhance search engine indexing.
4. **High-Quality Content**: Create valuable, engaging content that encourages shares and backlinks. High-quality content is more likely to be favoured by search engines and shared by users.
5. **Use Hashtags Strategically**: Use relevant and trending hashtags to increase the reach of your posts. Hashtags act as keywords on social media platforms, improving the discoverability of your content.
6. **Engage with Followers**: Regular interactions and responses to comments and messages can improve your engagement metrics, which search engines consider when ranking content.
7. **Cross-Promotion**: Share your social media content across various platforms and link to your profiles from your website and blog. This creates more entry points for search engines to index your content.

Monitoring and Adjustment

1. **Analytics Tools**: Use tools like Google Analytics, Facebook Insights, or Twitter Analytics to monitor the performance of your SEO efforts.
2. **Adjust Strategy**: Regularly review your analytics to identify which keywords and content strategies are most effective. Adjust your approach based on this data to continually improve your SEO.

Conclusion

Using SEO techniques to optimise your social media profiles and content enhances your discoverability, leading to increased visibility and engagement. By implementing keyword research, profile optimisation, and high-quality content creation, you can effectively improve your search engine rankings and attract more followers. Regularly monitoring your performance and adjusting your strategy ensures sustained growth and success in your social media efforts.

Chapter 17
Create Viral Content

Creating viral content is a powerful way to attract a massive audience and significantly boost your social media presence. Viral content spreads rapidly through shares, likes, and comments, reaching a wide audience in a short time. Here's a comprehensive summary of how to effectively create viral content.

Characteristics of Viral Content

1. **Emotional Appeal**: Content that evokes strong emotions such as joy, surprise, or awe is more likely to be shared. Aim to create content that resonates emotionally with your audience.
2. **Relatability**: Content that viewers can easily relate to and see themselves in tends to go viral. This includes everyday situations, common experiences, and universal themes.
3. **Shareability**: Ensure your content is easily shareable across platforms. Include clear calls to action encouraging viewers to share with their network.
4. **Visual Appeal**: High-quality visuals, including images and videos, attract attention and are more likely to be shared. Ensure your content is visually engaging and professionally presented.

Strategies for Creating Viral Content

1. **Know Your Audience**: Understand the preferences, interests, and behaviors of your target audience. Create content that aligns with their values and interests to increase the likelihood of shares.
2. **Create Compelling Headlines**: Craft attention-grabbing headlines that pique curiosity and encourage clicks. A strong headline is crucial in drawing viewers in.

3. **Use Trending Topics**: Incorporate current trends and popular topics into your content. Staying relevant increases the chances of your content being shared widely.
4. **Incorporate Humour**: Humor is a highly effective tool for making content shareable. Light-hearted, funny content often gets shared more frequently.
5. **Leverage User-Generated Content**: Encourage your audience to create and share content related to your brand. User-generated content adds authenticity and broadens your reach.
6. **Create Interactive Content**: Interactive content like polls, quizzes, and challenges engages viewers and encourages sharing. Participation increases the content's spread.
7. **Collaborate with Influencers**: Partner with influencers who have large followings. Their endorsement can significantly boost your content's visibility.

Promoting Your Content

1. **Cross-Platform Sharing**: Share your content across multiple social media platforms to maximize reach. Each platform has its unique audience and sharing dynamics.
2. **Engage with Your Audience**: Respond to comments, engage in discussions, and acknowledge shares. Active engagement increases visibility and encourages further sharing.
3. **Utilize Hashtags**: Use relevant and trending hashtags to increase the discoverability of your content. Hashtags help your content reach a broader audience.

Monitoring and Analysis

1. **Track Performance**: Use analytics tools to monitor the performance of your content. Metrics such as shares, likes, comments, and reach will help you understand what works best.
2. **Adjust Strategy**: Based on performance data, refine your content strategy. Focus on what resonates most with your audience to increase the chances of creating viral content.

Conclusion

Creating viral content involves crafting emotionally appealing, relatable, and shareable material. By understanding your audience, leveraging trends, and promoting your content effectively, you can maximise your chances of going viral. Engaging with your audience and continually refining your strategy based on analytics will help sustain and grow your social media presence.

Chapter 18
Monetise Live Streams

Monetising live streams is an effective way to engage with your audience in real-time and generate income through tips or donations. Live streaming allows for direct interaction, fostering a sense of community and loyalty among viewers.

Benefits of Monetising Live Streams

1. **Real-Time Engagement**: Live streams provide an immediate way to connect with your audience, answering questions and responding to comments on the spot.
2. **Increased Interaction**: The interactive nature of live streaming encourages more active participation from viewers, enhancing engagement and retention.
3. **Direct Revenue**: Platforms like YouTube, Twitch, and Facebook allow viewers to tip or donate during live streams, providing a direct source of income.

Strategies for Successful Live Streams

1. **Choose the Right Platform**: Select a platform that aligns with your audience's preferences. YouTube and Facebook are suitable for broad audiences, while Twitch caters more to gaming and niche interests.
2. **Plan Your Content**: Structure your live streams with a clear plan or agenda. Whether it's a Q&A session, a tutorial, or a behind-the-scenes look, having a focus keeps viewers engaged.
3. **Promote Your Live Streams**: Announce your live streams in advance across your social media channels to build anticipation. Use eye-catching visuals and engaging posts to attract viewers.

4. **Engage with Viewers**: Actively engage with your audience by addressing comments, answering questions, and acknowledging donations. Personal interaction makes viewers feel valued and more likely to contribute.
5. **Offer Incentives**: Encourage tips and donations by offering incentives, such as shoutouts, exclusive content, or entry into giveaways. Clear call-to-actions can prompt viewers to support your stream.

Maximizing Earnings

1. **Utilise Platform Features**: Take advantage of platform-specific features like YouTube's Super Chat, Twitch's Bits and Subscriptions, or Facebook Stars. These tools make it easy for viewers to tip or donate.
2. **Collaborate with Brands**: Partner with brands for sponsored live streams. This can provide additional income and add value to your content.
3. **Promote Merchandise**: Use your live streams to promote your own products or merchandise. Offering exclusive discounts or bundles during the stream can drive sales.

Conclusion

Monetising live streams leverages real-time engagement to build a loyal community and generate income. By choosing the right platform, planning engaging content, and actively interacting with viewers, you can maximize tips and donations. Utilizing platform features and collaborating with brands further enhances your earning potential, making live streaming a valuable component of your social media strategy.

Chapter 19
Write Sponsored Blog Posts

Writing sponsored blog posts is a lucrative way to earn additional income by collaborating with brands. Here's a concise summary of how to effectively integrate sponsored posts into your blogging strategy.

Benefits of Sponsored Blog Posts

1. **Additional Income**: Sponsored posts provide a direct revenue stream, with brands paying you to write content promoting their products or services.
2. **Content Diversity**: Collaborating with brands introduces new content ideas and topics, keeping your blog fresh and engaging.

Strategies for Effective Sponsored Posts

1. **Choose Relevant Brands**: Partner with brands that align with your blog's niche and audience. Authenticity is key; your readers should find the sponsored content valuable and relevant.
2. **Disclose Sponsorship**: Transparently disclose sponsored content to maintain trust with your audience. Honesty about partnerships is essential for credibility.
3. **Create High-Quality Content**: Ensure sponsored posts are well-written and provide genuine value. Blend the promotional content naturally within informative or entertaining posts.
4. **Engage Your Audience**: Encourage interaction by asking for feedback or opinions on the sponsored product. Engaging readers enhances the effectiveness of the post.

Promoting Sponsored Posts

1. **Use Social Media**: Promote your sponsored posts across your social media channels to increase visibility and reach.
2. **SEO Optimisation**: Optimize your posts with relevant keywords to improve search engine rankings and attract organic traffic.

Conclusion

Sponsored blog posts offer a viable way to monetise your blog while adding valuable content. By partnering with relevant brands, maintaining transparency, and creating high-quality content, you can effectively integrate sponsored posts into your blogging strategy and enhance your income.

Chapter 20

Attend Social Media Workshops

Attending social media workshops and webinars is an excellent way to stay current with the latest trends and strategies in the ever-evolving digital landscape. These events provide valuable insights, practical skills, and networking opportunities that can significantly enhance your social media presence and effectiveness.

Benefits of Attending Social Media Workshops

1. **Stay Updated**: Social media is constantly changing, with new tools, algorithms, and trends emerging regularly. Workshops and webinars keep you informed about the latest developments, ensuring your strategies remain relevant and effective.
2. **Learn from Experts**: These events often feature industry experts and influencers who share their knowledge and experience. Learning from those at the forefront of social media can provide you with advanced techniques and innovative ideas.
3. **Practical Skills**: Workshops typically offer hands-on training, allowing you to practice new skills and tools in a supportive environment. This practical approach helps you apply what you learn directly to your social media efforts.
4. **Networking Opportunities**: Attending workshops and webinars provides a platform to connect with other professionals in your field. Building relationships with peers, influencers, and potential collaborators can open up new opportunities for growth and collaboration.

Strategies for Maximizing Workshop Benefits

1. **Choose Relevant Topics**: Select workshops and webinars that align with your specific needs and goals. Focus on areas where you seek improvement or want to explore new opportunities.
2. **Active Participation**: Engage actively during the sessions by asking questions, participating in discussions, and taking notes. Active involvement enhances your learning experience and helps you retain information better.
3. **Implement What You Learn**: Apply the strategies and techniques you learn as soon as possible. Experimenting with new ideas and

tools on your social media platforms helps solidify your understanding and improve your skills.

4. **Follow Up**: Stay in touch with speakers and fellow attendees. Follow them on social media, join related online groups, and continue the conversation beyond the workshop. This ongoing engagement can lead to valuable insights and collaborations.

Finding Workshops and Webinars

1. **Industry Organizations**: Look for workshops hosted by reputable industry organizations and associations. These events are often well-structured and provide high-quality content.
2. **Social Media Platforms**: Platforms like Facebook, LinkedIn, and Twitter frequently promote relevant workshops and webinars. Following industry leaders and groups can help you stay informed about upcoming events.
3. **Online Learning Platforms**: Websites like Coursera, Udemy, and Skillshare offer a variety of workshops and courses on social media marketing and strategy.

Conclusion

Attending social media workshops and webinars is essential for keeping up-to-date with the latest trends and strategies. By learning from experts, gaining practical skills, and networking with peers, you can enhance your social media efforts and stay ahead in the dynamic digital landscape. Select relevant events, actively participate, and implement new techniques to maximize the benefits of these learning opportunities.